Ernest W. Watson's
SKETCH DIARY

A Venetian Canal. Pencil Drawing.

Ernest W. Watson's
SKETCH DIARY

*with instructive text on brush
and pencil techniques*

 REINHOLD PUBLISHING CORPORATION / NEW YORK

This book is dedicated to my wife Eve, good companion on many trips recorded by the sketches on these pages. Intrepid critic, fervent appreciator of every worthy scrap of my drawings, sketches and writings, she has typed all the manuscripts and proofread all the galleys for my last nine books.

Published in the United States of America 1965 by
Reinhold Publishing Corporation, 430 Park Avenue, New York, N.Y.
All Rights Reserved
Library of Congress Catalog Card Number: 65-12979
Type Set by Graphic Arts Typographers, Inc.
Printed and bound in Tokyo, Japan, by Zokeisha Publications, Limited
Designed by Ernest W. Watson

Preface

For years it has been my practice to record many of the places I have been and the things I have seen in small sketchbooks that I carry with me in my travels at home and abroad. I think of these sketchbooks as pictorial diaries. Like the entries in a written diary, each small sketch recalls a particular time and place, and many are associated with very pleasant personal experiences. A number of the illustrations in this book, for example, were selected from the book I call "Eve's Sketchbook." It was begun in 1950, soon after our marriage, and is a pictorial record of our wanderings together.

Friends who have enjoyed leafing through my sketch diaries have often suggested that others would be interested in seeing the sketches and in learning of the simple procedures I follow in doing them. The purpose of this book, therefore, is to introduce others to the pleasures that I have found in sketching, and to encourage the reader to go and do likewise. In many previous books I have focused upon techniques, but in this book the technical aspects of drawing and painting are only touched upon. The emphasis is chiefly on picturemaking and on simple ways of solving the problems the reader may encounter in creating his own pictorial diary.

With the exception of a few demonstration drawings, the illustrations have all been selected from my own sketch diaries. For me they represent something of a sentimental journey in time. It is my hope that for the reader they will be a stimulation to his own creative desires.

Ernest W. Watson

Cottage #1, Rustic Canyon, California. The subject of this pen·sketch is the cottage at the Huntington Hartford Foundation in Rustic Canyon, Pacific Palisades, California, which my wife and I occupied during residence Fellowships in the winter of 1962.

Contents

TEMPERANCEVILLE MD
June 27 1960
On return from Virginia Beach

Old House, Temperanceville, Maryland. Two versions of the same subject in Temperanceville, Maryland, show contrasting techniques of line and tone. The line drawing, opposite page, is a fifteen minute sketch made the first time I drove past the house and was attracted by its interesting structure. Years later, on a return trip north from Virginia Beach, I was again stopped by the subject. This time I rendered it in tone, spending perhaps three-quarters of an hour doing it. In the tonal sketch, above, I tried to represent the dramatic aspect of the blackened clapboards which had never seen a coat of paint. In the first sketch I had cheated a little by omitting one of the four sections which are put together in a manner that is characteristic of both old and newer houses in the area. The suggestion of the roadside gives support and perspective to the tonal sketch.

temperanceville maryland 1955
15 minute Sketch

The Sketch Diary

The first thing to remember in starting a pictorial diary is that you are not competing with a camera. At times you may want to identify a subject as accurately as possible, but in creating a sketchbook diary it is usually of far greater importance to record an experience, using it as a *theme,* as a vehicle for remembrance.

Now *theme* in music is "a short melody constituting the basis of variation, development and the like." It seems to me that is a good definition of the kind of sketching we have in mind here, the kind of sketching that presumably you will want in your pictorial diary. It suggests the dominance of feeling over factual copying. It suggests a creative approach and freedom of expression. It implies the kinds of sketches which years later can recreate the joy you had in the places that inspired them. Any sketch you make of a place that gives you a rewarding experience holds within it the recollection of every pleasant detail of the entire day. If perchance *you* have kept a picture diary I do not need to stress this most rewarding aspect of this type of sketchbook. You have already proved to yourself that a picture is worth a lot more than a thousand words..

"Variation and development of a theme" implies liberty to interpret or translate facts with whatever pictorial competence you have at your command. The exact proportion of a building, or tree, or whatever it is, is of less significance than the melody you have made of it in your sketchbook. Your sketch may be out of drawing, the perspective somewhat cockeyed and other aspects of the scene violated —but there still can be melody and life in it.

Well, what if your drawing skill is limited, as indeed it is with any beginner? How can one exercise such freedom without a marked degree of facility in pictorial language?

One of the best answers that comes to mind is found in the drawings of the late Hendrick Willem Van Loon with which he illustrated many of his fascinating books. I have a copy of his *The Arts* (Simon and Schuster) on my desk as I write, and I implore the reader to secure a copy to serve as a demonstration of what I have just been saying. As an artist, Van Loon remained an amateur. His illustrations are seldom correct in perspective or proportion, his figure drawings are no more sophisticated. Yet he fearlessly tackled almost every subject mentioned in his text. He sketched the architectural glories of Greece and Rome, the Taj Mahal and the Brooklyn Bridge. In such drawings he achieved a kind of eloquence that springs from love, enthusiasm and daring. His drawings are a kind of picture writing. Technical proficiency is of course a good thing, but it does not necessarily guarantee eloquence or charm.

Now any student who examines Van Loon's sketches will better understand the point I am making—that anyone who is unafraid can acquire enough proficiency to make satisfying pictorial notes of whatever he may wish to preserve in a sketchbook diary. And, again, Van Loon's illustrations should assure the amateur that his own sketches, though crude at first, can be of more value to him than snapshots he might make with his camera.

How can this be so? When you click the shutter of your camera you capture a complete picture of the object or scene. But you have not *seen* it as you would have if you had sat down with pencil or brush and made a drawing of it. And the photo will not have the same meaning for you as would the drawing. If you make a drawing of the scene, you will have *really* seen it, seen its essence. There is a vast difference of experience when we draw an object or scene which inspires us. Our vision then is penetrating, discerning. We examine the scene with the utmost perception. We analyze our interest in it, we determine what aspect of it is of personal interest to us, and we focus upon this in our sketch. Thus we fasten our love upon it. In a very real sense we become a part of it and it becomes a part of us. There is a kind of reciprocal communication here that is familiar enough to the artist. It may seem a metaphysical concept to others. Indeed it is just that. Consider for example the difference of feeling you have in drawing from nature and in drawing from photographs. Drawing as simple an object as a jug gives one a more meaningful emotion than working from a photograph of the most interesting subject. When artist and object coexist in the same scene, are breathing the same atmosphere, so to speak, there is a vital sense of intimacy with the object of interest.

Perhaps this phenomenon cannot be made clear to the layman, but in large measure it explains the value of an amateur's drawing, even though he may not quite understand it or even wonder about it. So the beginner has to take this promise on faith and await the discovery of its reality in his own experience.

There are other approaches to the seeing process which I will touch upon later. But I do want to begin this book upon the note I've been stressing, because I assume that readers will be taking up sketching for love rather than for money. And I am thinking particularly of those who will be carrying sketchbooks on their journeys as I do.

My sketchbooks, incidentally, are relatively small. Most of the sketches shown in this book are reproduced at the exact size of the originals. Small books are more convenient to carry and small drawings and watercolors are more quickly made. There is an advantage in this. Time is often pressing and there may be other restricting conditions. When you are traveling you may, during a single day, come upon many interesting subjects which you want to record in your sketchbook. A few years ago while driving through Georgia and the Carolinas, for example, I was intrigued by the quaint little churches along the way. During the entire day I concentrated upon these churches. Three of those sketches will be found in this book. Each took but a few minutes—except for the Huspah Baptist Church in Yemassee, South Carolina, which lured me inside to make interior sketches.

For practical reasons most of my sketches when traveling are done with lead pencils. They are the simplest tools to carry about and they can give rapid results. But some of my books are almost entirely filled with watercolors. These also can be done quickly in small scale with limited equipment. They present an infinitely simpler technical problem than large-scale watercolors which are indeed frightening to many beginners. The procedures for painting watercolor miniatures are briefly discussed in the section on watercolor sketching, and can readily be learned by any serious student.

I have made a point of the satisfactions of sketching for those who have had scant training in drawing, but of course the more sound art training one has, the more satisfying will be the results in those sketchbook drawings. There are many books on perspective, composition and technical procedures, including some I have written myself, which the serious student will consult as a matter of course. In many areas such books will be available at the nearest public library.

Pattern

Whenever you set down two masses of tone or color, however simple, you create pattern. It may not be especially good or interesting pattern, but pattern it is. In sketching, or in picturemaking of any kind, you cannot escape pattern. At first you may not pay much attention to it, and your sketches may be satisfying records of your subjects even so, because composition is less important in some subjects than in others. However, with the development of skill you will become increasingly conscious of pattern, a purely abstract quality which contributes artistic value to whatever you do.

Pattern of course refers to the shapes and sizes of pictorial elements and to their relative positions in the compositional arrangement. Values—dark and light tones—are also a factor. I have purposely eliminated value differences in the flat analysis of the Wellfleet subject, opposite below, because I wanted to put the emphasis there upon shapes and positions. Those clumps of grasses growing out of the mud are nearly as I saw them when sketching, but not quite. I shifted them about some in order to improve their pattern arrangement. As you develop a compositional sense, you will do this automatically. Exact faithfulness to the subject's details is usually unimportant; it can even be uninteresting.

The lighted areas of the background tree masses in this sketch are likewise somewhat arbitrary. However, they do in a general way suggest the actual character of the foliage arrangement on the hill as I saw it.

The scene represents a backwater of Wellfleet Harbor. At the time I sketched it, the tide was out. What was water during the high tide was now an expanse of wet mud in which those clumps of grasses were rooted. To have copied the dark value of the mud would have been out of the question in a pencil sketch, and it was natural to render the shiny wetness of the mud as white paper. The same procedure might have been followed if a high tide had filled the basin with water. Perhaps then the sunlight on the water would have presented a light surface.

One quickly learns how effective white paper can be when working in pencil or pen. In these mediums it is usually better to avoid large dark masses and to make the paper do much of the work. The Strathmore Paper Company once made good use of the slogan, "Paper is part of the picture." It is a good slogan for the sketcher to remember. Think of the sketch as a shorthand rendering that avoids the effort of facsimile representation.

My *pattern analysis* of course omits technical effects which are important in the sketch. The direction of pencil strokes, for instance, is essential in revealing the character of every detail—and good tech-

Wellfleet Backwater, Cape Cod, Massachusetts.

nique is charming in itself. Stroke direction is something that is always a problem for a beginner who may have to resort to mere scumbling before he develops any degree of technical facility. This should not be discouraging. Keep remembering the purpose of those diary sketches; they are intended as pleasant reminders which have to satisfy no one but yourself. Even one's first rather crude attempts will do that, and improvement grows with practice.

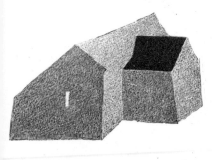

Values

The function of values is perhaps best emphasized by reference to the absence thereof in the pattern analysis of the Wellfleet Harbor sketch on the preceding page. In that analysis, all masses are resolved into a single flat tone in order to dramatize just one aspect of composition in picturemaking. The analysis reveals effectively the function of pattern insofar as shapes and their disposition in the scene are concerned. It also points up the need for value modulation, not only for giving the impression of reality but, equally important, for esthetic stimulation.

The diagrams on these pages are intended to demonstrate both the practical and the abstract functions of value diversification. Figures 1, 2 and 3 on page 15 reveal the increasing contribution of value diversification in clarifying the facts of the scene and in providing more esthetic pleasure. In figure 4 the addition of value gradation enlarges the range of visual excitation. The figures to the left on this page are the value opposites of figures 1, 2, 3 and 4 on page 15. In value contrasts we have the means for dramatic expression in even the simplest subjects.

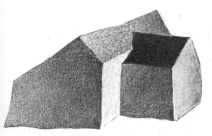

Tonal gradation offers an almost unlimited opportunity for illustrative emphasis. By tonal manipulation the artist can focus attention upon any part of his picture. There is a suggestion of this in figure 5 where interest is focused just where it is wanted; in this instance upon the nearest corner of the barn and around the door.

Since we are more conscious of values when they are seen in mass, this demonstration may seem to refer specifically to painting. But value relationships are of equal concern in a pencil or pen sketch, even though they may be more subtle. In the pencil sketch at Rockland, Maine, on page 57, note how the gradation from light to dark focuses interest upon the ships. The pencil sketch of St. Ives Harbor on page 17 encompasses the distant town as well as the immediate foreground, and one is automatically committed to the greatest possible range of values. On the other hand, in the delicate sketch of the wheat field at Salisbury, Maryland, on page 25, the value range had to be both limited and subtle. A penline drawing like that made in Rustic Canyon (page 6) depends upon other compositional factors more than upon value, although even here the need for tonal focus is satisfied in the rendering of the cottage. In almost every sketch there is a need for emphasis somewhere by means of value diversification. The ability to see this need and to provide for it comes naturally with the development of technical facility.

Foregrounds

I think of a foreground as the threshold over which one enters the picture. Not every sketch seems to need such an entrance, but as you leaf through this book you will note that frequently an interesting foreground treatment gives support as well as an invitation to the body of the sketch. This is the case in the drawing on page 17 of boats stranded by low tide on the sand at St. Ives Harbor. In this subject, as in many others, foreground shapes had to be arbitrarily designed rather than copied from what wasn't there to copy. That St. Ives beach was an almost unbroken flat tone. The light and dark masses of the sketch were designed to create what I felt was an interesting pattern. Note that those patches of penciled tones are mainly horizontal, a series of steps as it were, leading into the picture, while lines of cables from anchors driven in the sand carry the eye back into the distance.

The foregrounds of the Wellfleet Harbor scene, page 13, and that of Rockland Harbor, page 57, serve more as walls, separating the foregrounds from the middle distances. Where there is a road leading into the picture, as in the sketches of Guilford, Vermont, page 47, and Sabino Canyon, page 63, the linear perspective of the roadsides carries the eye into the distance. By contrast, note the absence of foreground in the sketches of the dying tree, page 56, the stack of cartwheels, page 49, and the one-pony ranch, page 28. It is all a matter of feeling that there is or there isn't a need for foreground. It's an individual choice, and you can't always give a good reason for the choice. The point is that when foreground is wanted, its rendering is as much a matter of design as of illustration. Refer, for example, to the sketch on page 20 of the little church with the pyramidal spire. The plank bridge over the ditch, the sides of the ditch and the empty drums are interesting illustrative accompaniments which give opportunity for suitable disposition of masses and lines. Another artist might well have disposed them in another way. In my sketch they offer good support and entrance into the churchyard.

TIDE OUT. ST. IVES
Cornwall England

Tide Out, St. Ives, Cornwall, England. I made many sketches at St. Ives, which is one of Cornwall's most famous fishing ports. The fishing boats are anchored near shore while the tide is in, and are left there to settle on the sand when the tide goes out. They are then accessible to the carts into which the catch is unloaded. Some subjects are in themselves well-composed pictures as was this scene. The ships supply the focal point, and the stone wharf provides a strong middle distance that reaches back into the town. The more distant environs of the town, sketched with delicacy, stretch up the hill and meet the sky. The treatment of the foreground is discussed in the text. The drawing was made with three degrees of pencil leads, the softest providing the dark of the boats, the hardest giving suitable light tones for the distant areas.

Light And Shade

There are two ways of representing two-dimensional objects: (1) by light and shadow; (2) by linear perspective. We do not see objects in linear terms. Line is an arbitrary, a symbolic device for representing shapes that are defined by contrasting values and colors in nature.

In considering how light defines form, imagine the ancient gray barns on the opposite page as they would appear if we approached them very early on a misty morning. In the misty half-light they would be seen as a simple silhouetted mass, without three-dimensional appearance. With the sun's rising, structure would begin to emerge dimly, but the light might not be bright enough to reveal details, except for some dark shapes that would be recognized as openings. Then, as the mist evaporated and the sun brightened, form would stand forth in sharply defined light and shade, and details could be seen clearly.

If the roof were brilliantly illuminated, it might well appear as light in value as the sky. In that case, unless there were darker masses behind the barn to provide a contrast in values that would define the shape of the roof, we would be forced to make use of line to indicate the ridge line in our sketch. Of course in sketching we habitually do rely upon line in rendering much of any drawing, even when tone predominates. Line even may serve to emphasize an edge where light and dark meet.

Shadows that are created by bright light are important in defining the forms which cast them. They also provide the basis for pattern interest. The illustration at the bottom of page 19 is a light-and-shadow analysis of the watercolor sketch of the farmhouse reproduced in color on page 36. The analysis in black ink demonstrates how a simple shadow pattern can serve as a useful basis for any rendering, either in black-and-white mass or in color. The time of day, and hence the sun's position, is an important factor in determining such light-and-shadow patterns. Evidently in this case the sun was in a most advantageous position for sketching purposes.

A group of old barns as they might appear in the very early light of a misty morning.

As the fog lifts somewhat and the light brightens, the forms begin to emerge.

In the bright sun and clear atmosphere, strong light and shade reveal details as values become more varied.

Shadow diagram of the watercolor subject reproduced in color on page 36. Shadows not only define form, they very often provide compositional interest. The simpler in value the shadow pattern, the more dramatic the picture.

Somewhere in S. Carolina

Jun 1955

Beach Hill Baptist Church
Georgia   near Midway

Huspah Baptist Church,
Yemassee S.C.   Jan 26 1955

Three Churches, South Carolina. One day in South Carolina
I made several pencil sketches of little churches, three are
shown above and on the facing page. Many of them were
deserted; all of them displayed the imaginations of amateur
architects. The Huspah Baptist Church at Yemassee (above)
was one of the more ambitious buildings. The live oak tree
draped with Spanish moss seemed to hover protectively over
it. Tree and church made a most appealing subject. The
church appeared to be still in use.

Old Houses
on Via Porta Pinciana
ROME
view from my hotel window

Old Houses on Via Porta Pinciana, Rome. View from my hotel window. Like so many drawings one makes in a sketch diary, this view from my hotel window in Rome does not represent a tourist attraction—except for one tourist. It is included in this collection because it combines foliage with the brilliant sunlight-and-shadow effect of an early morning.

On the Road to Charleston. Driving along Route 17 in South Carolina, not far from the Atlantic coast, one comes upon lovely avenues of live oaks and other trees. Sometimes they arch over the road, as in this pencil sketch. I was especially interested here in the Spanish moss which drapes the branches and foliage of the trees in a way that suggests falling water. The miniature one-tone analysis of this subject was made to emphasize the importance of unifying pattern in the composition of a sketch.

The Sky

First let me assure you that it is practically impossible to invent cloud shapes which are not duplicated in nature. Clouds tossed about by erratic winds sometimes assume almost unbelievable forms. If you take a soft piece of charcoal and mess around on a piece of textured paper, then rub with your thumb or fingers, you will produce something that resembles a stormy sky. If then with a piece of kneaded eraser you pick out some white shapes, you will be surprised at how easily you can design some very plausible cloud masses. This is a good exercise to practice. All the while you should be observing clouds in the sky, becoming familiar with the characteristic forms most commonly seen. (You'll find them described and classified in your encyclopedia.) But, as I've promised, you will by accident alone—playing with charcoal masses—come up with cloud forms you can use.

As you sketch clouds, whether in line or mass, you will develop a personal technique. At first you may do little more than scumble. And when you do that you will be in good company, as you will discover in studying drawings and etchings by very competent artists. We all develop individual techniques. When indicating shadows in my sketches I am apt to employ a right-to-left downward stroke, such as is naturally made by the right hand in a writing position. Like others, I seem to have developed something of a formula. Sometimes I stick in a few flying birds, dark against the sky, to help give the illusion of space.

But the sky is nothing to worry about. Often you may not feel the need of it in your diary sketches. Running through my own sketchbooks, I find that more often than not I have neglected the sky altogether, or I have been satisfied with the barest linear cloud suggestion. In *painting* one usually feels more of a need for cloud forms, as you will note in many of my watercolor sketches. In pencil work, however, we rely principally on line, and the simplest kind of cloud treatment will ordinarily be adequate. Whether you use horizontal shapes or shapes suggestive of cumulus clouds will depend upon the compositional needs of your subject.

Remember that when you deem clouds essential to your sketch —and you will not always want them—they should be a significant part of the over-all composition. In the Assisi street scene on page 59, note how the sky and the buildings are unified by the flowing together of the dark cloud and the shadow on the wall. This unity of sky and land is something that you will master as you continue your study.

Wheat Field, from our Motel Window, Salisbury, Maryland. This pencil sketch focuses more upon the sky than upon the wheat field. It records a glorious June day when cumulus clouds boiled up over an almost unbroken horizon. The pattern of white shapes in the wheat field breaks up what otherwise would be an uninterrupted and monotonous gray covering. The result probably doesn't particularly look like a wheat field!

A Word About Techniques

Every creative person has a special aptitude for a specific type of artistic expression. In the visual arts this aptitude is usually reflected in the choice of medium. One artist becomes a sculptor, another a painter, a designer or a graphic artist. Narrowing the field to drawing or sketching mediums, there is still room for choice, a preference for one tool or another. It may be ink, charcoal, wash, watercolor, drybrush or pencil. This is not to say that one must be imprisoned within the scope of any single medium. Indeed the creative person usually seeks many outlets for his varied impulses. Yet there is likely to be a favored tool or medium with which one feels more at home and in which his capacities find most satisfying fruition.

Although I have worked extensively with other mediums, I have done more with the pencil than with any other drawing tool. How one is led to a particular medium seems often to be a matter of chance. While I was a student in art school, a framed pencil drawing by the late Charles H. Woodbury—he was a notable painter, etcher and teacher—fascinated me and led me irresistibly in a direction, it seems, I could not escape. At any rate, I found myself earning much of my living through the pencil, doing illustrations and advertisements, and teaching pencil sketching.

Of course the pencil is the most convenient of all mediums for the sketching artist. A handful of pencils of varying degrees of hardness, a kneaded eraser, a variety of papers, and a portfolio which can serve as drawing board as well as the carrier of finished sketches comprise the entire outfit, except perhaps for a folding camp stool—and an automobile or airplane to get you about.

Fountain pens are equally handy, now that they have been designed to carry India ink as well as writing ink. And when you come down to convenience, it is possible for the sketcher to manage small watercolors with the scant equipment described in the next chapter.

Another convenient drawing tool is the relatively new felt tip pen. Actually it is more like a brush than a pen. In my sketch of a Wyoming butte on the facing page you can see how the felt tip will effectively render large dark masses in a brushlike manner. However, the delicate penlike strokes, in places, demonstrate the possibilities of this tool for sensitive detail as well. This is a rather tricky medium because the flow of ink—a dye, really—is rather difficult to control. It is a fine disciplinary tool since corrections are impossible. What you put down, stays.

I think every beginner ought to experiment with many tools and mediums. He should not only learn which is his special tool, but should acquire the courage to use whatever others will best do a particular job.

One must not overlook the importance of paper. The selection of improper paper accounts for more failures than improper handling of the medium. In teaching I have always found it difficult to get this truth across. Students somehow seem assured that any paper labeled pencil paper, charcoal paper or watercolor paper is certain to be satisfactory for the indicated purpose. This is far from the case. You simply have to experiment and experiment, forgetting the labels manufacturers put on their products, and make your own discoveries.

a Wyoming Butte

A Wyoming Butte. This sketch was drawn with a felt tip pen, a relatively new tool that is also referred to as a felt brush or simply a felt tip. It can be used to render large dark masses with brushlike strokes, but it is also capable of delicate pen-like strokes.

ONE PONY RANCH
ON LA JOLLA SCENIC DRIVE
CAL.

One-Pony Ranch on the La Jolla, California, Scenic Drive.
This cozy little corral and barn, on the crest of Scenic Drive,
has a variety of picturesque aspects that drew me to it—the
shape of the barn, the jumbled corral fences and that graceful tree at the left which looks like a willow but isn't. The
place overlooks a broad valley which I indicated only by a
line. No foreground seemed indicated here since the structure is close to the road.

Papago Indian Farmhouse, on the Road to Spanish Mission
San Xavier, near Tucson, Arizona.

INDIAN HOUSE NEAR MISSION SAN XAVIER, TUCSON

Sketching With Watercolor

Since it is not the function of this book to offer detailed technical instruction in watercolor or any other medium, I suggest that those readers who are not already familiar with basic watercolor techniques consult one or more of the excellent texts available before attempting to paint color miniatures in sketchbooks. Rex Brandt's *Watercolor Technique in 15 Lessons* (Reinhold) is a small and inexpensive text that is particularly useful for those who require instruction in the essentials of this medium. It demonstrates what one can accomplish with very limited palettes, an important consideration for the particular kind of painting that is discussed here.

Once you have gained some familiarity with watercolors and ways of handling them you will find that painting miniatures in a sketchbook is much simpler than painting large-scale watercolors. The problems of stretching paper, running large washes, controlling color in large areas, and many other technical matters are not encountered. Nor is there a need for elaborate equipment. Entirely satisfactory results are obtained with a few colors and with such materials as can be carried in pocket or handbag. There are on the market small watercolor boxes that measure no more than 3 x 5 inches when folded. The metal box holds eight tubes of paint and three short-handled sable brushes; and the two hinged covers, one folding over the other, form palettes for mixing colors. This is an excellent palette box, yet one can very well get along without it. The five or six tubes of color that suffice for watercolor sketching can be carried in a pocket.

Of course some kind of palette for mixing is necessary. Plastic palettes without covers are available with six or eight cups for holding paint and much larger mixing areas than are provided by the small, complete, folding boxes above mentioned. The larger the mixing space the better; colors are apt to become unintentionally mingled on very small palettes. Disposable palettes are also practical. They can be purchased in art supply stores, or can be cut to size from stiff white cardboard with a non-absorbent surface. The palette ought to be 12 inches long if possible in order to keep the colors well separated. Since such small amounts of color need to be squeezed onto the palette for a sketch or two, the leftover pigments can be discarded along with the palette. Next time, one begins with fresh color on a new palette.

So-called school colors in tubes are inexpensive and may satisfy many users, but such small amounts are needed for miniatures that it is small economy to use other than the best colors attainable. Excellent dry colors of good manufacture also come in cake form and some artists prefer them. They have the advantage of being ready for use without the bother of squeezing color from tubes, but unlike tube colors they require a little time for softening before releasing their full color strength.

Although the best sable brushes are expensive, they last a long time if properly cleaned after use, and it does not pay to use cheap brushes which will not perform well. The diagram on page 31 illustrates the approximate sizes of sable brushes that are most useful for small-scale sketching. A flat bristle brush about one-quarter inch wide can be used both for applying color and for scrubbing out parts that need correcting. For removing color, wet the brush, gently scrub, then blot with a cloth. The corrective color can be applied when the area has dried.

A soft cotton cloth should always be handy for blotting. It is especially useful for absorbing color that is too dark before the color sets. An ink eraser can also be used to lighten a color that is too dark in value—but only in a very small area and after the color is bone dry. A small piece of very soft nylon sponge is useful at times. When moistened, it will lift off color neatly. This is especially helpful in painting skies when a white cloud is wanted within a sky color which still is moist. Needless to say, one should experiment with all these things to acquire skill in their use.

If you work on loose sheets of paper rather than in a sketchbook, you will need some kind of support. A small portfolio will serve this purpose, and will also carry paper and finished paintings.

Light metal and canvas sketching stools are available in most art stores. It is best to have one of them along even when you expect to sketch from your car. Often you will want a different vantage point than the car seat provides.

The choice of paper is of utmost importance. It should not have a surface that is too smooth, yet it should not be heavily textured since small-scale watercolors call for rather fine detail. The paper ought to be reasonably heavy, however. Examine sketchbooks found in art stores and try out two or three in order to find the paper which is most receptive to color. Regular watercolor paper in sheets or in pads is available in many sizes. When working on a pad, no other support is needed. Large loose sheets can be cut down to whatever size you desire. The more you use watercolor in small or large scale, the more particular you will be about paper, which is indeed "part of the picture."

The simplest kind of watercolor sketch is like that reproduced on page 35. This is a fine line pen drawing which defines most, though not all, of the color masses. Note that the colors are all very gray. I made no effort here to copy the exact colors of the subject. The light tints on the tree masses have little color likeness to the dark greens of the foliage I saw. The cloud was painted with Payne's gray brightened a little with cobalt blue. This sketch is colored in a purely arbitrary

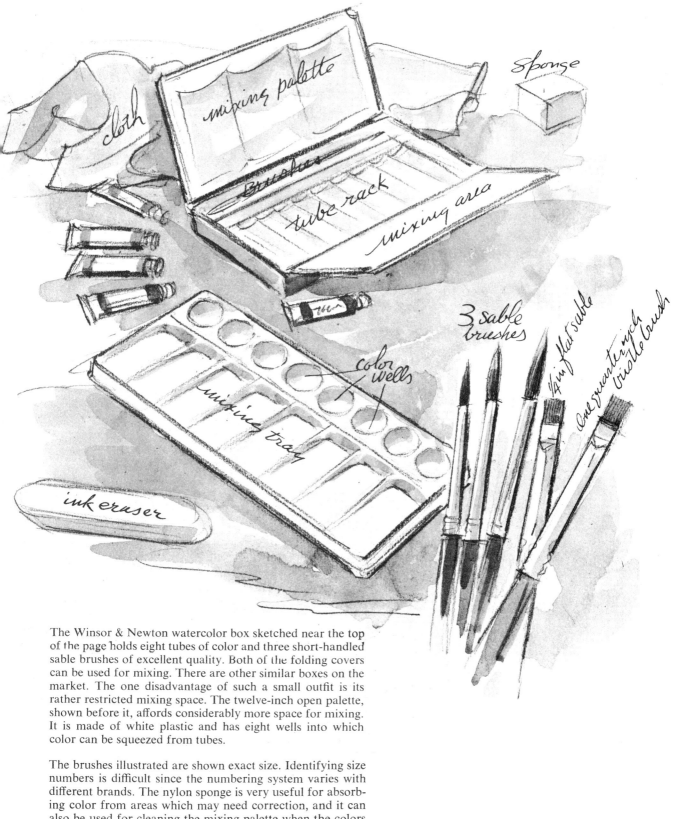

The Winsor & Newton watercolor box sketched near the top of the page holds eight tubes of color and three short-handled sable brushes of excellent quality. Both of the folding covers can be used for mixing. There are other similar boxes on the market. The one disadvantage of such a small outfit is its rather restricted mixing space. The twelve-inch open palette, shown before it, affords considerably more space for mixing. It is made of white plastic and has eight wells into which color can be squeezed from tubes.

The brushes illustrated are shown exact size. Identifying size numbers is difficult since the numbering system varies with different brands. The nylon sponge is very useful for absorbing color from areas which may need correction, and it can also be used for cleaning the mixing palette when the colors have become too intermingled. The ink eraser is sometimes used to lighten a color after it has become thoroughly dry on the paper.

manner but it serves its purpose for me. It represents the kind of color painting that can be done by anyone who has a modicum of drawing and painting skill.

The street scene on page 33 combines grayed orange washes with lead pencil. Any color added to a pencil drawing should be quite gray and very light in value. If the color is too assertive, either in hue or in value, it subordinates the pencil lines and tones unpleasantly. Color combines much more easily with pen line.

In full-color painting the beginner's most common difficulty is in the use of bright colors. Start with grayed colors. Then a touch of bright color can be added here and there to enliven the sketch. Of course there are exceptions, each subject having its own color needs, but if you keep thinking of your sketch as a suggestion rather than a literal transcript, you are likely to be better satisfied with the result. With increasing skill you can be more adventurous.

In *Watercolor Technique in 15 Lessons* Rex Brandt offers a low-key minimum palette of yellow ochre, burnt sienna and ivory black, the black substituting for blue. This limits one to a very gray scheme, but it is worth trying. I prefer Payne's gray to ivory black in such a palette because it has a bluish tinge. One can obtain a restrained color ensemble using three primaries such as cadmium yellow medium, alizarin crimson and ultramarine blue, provided the scheme is kept on the gray side in mixing. Naturally, it's a good idea to experiment with a wide variety of colors in the studio, using a text on watercolor techniques and color mixing as a guide.

The use of opaque color—color made opaque by the addition of Chinese white—is seldom cricket in large-scale watercolor painting unless the whole picture is frankly done in gouache technique. However, there's no need to be squeamish about using it in miniatures. I often use it along with transparent washes, not always, but whenever it serves my purpose. Sometimes in painting a transparent wash one loses light shapes or accents that are important, but they can be added easily with opaque color painted right over the dark areas when dry.

I have often been asked about the use of colored pencils or crayons for making color sketches. The answer is that colored pencils are a drawing medium rather than a painting medium, and do not give the full rich color effects of even a gray-toned watercolor. Crayon drawings rub easily and, like pencils, they lack the fluid quality of brushwork.

Via Degli Aramari, Assisi. This street, which leads under the arch to the famous church of St. Francis of Assisi, is rendered rather meticulously with pencil and a very gray burnt sienna wash. One has to be careful in combining wash with pencil to keep the color very light and gray in value; otherwise the color will subordinate the pencil work unpleasantly. Compare this drawing with the one on page 59, a rapid ink sketch with a gray wash.

VIA
DEGLI ARAMARI
ASSISI

OLD HOUSES ON HOUSTON STREET NEW YORK

Old Houses on Houston Street, New York. These three houses remained after others in the row had been torn down. The colors on the gable end represent what once were painted rooms of the adjoining house. The pink hue seen in places on the long side was achieved by drybrushing Chinese white over the rose-colored bricks.

Manasquan N.J.
June 25 1950

Bridge at Manasquan, New Jersey. This charming old wood drawbridge, sketched in 1950, has given way to progress; one more picturesque subject gone the way of so many attractions of a quieter age. The day must have been sunny to give such definite shadows under the bridge.

Old House and Sheds. This pen-and-watercolor sketch, reduced in size from the original which is nine inches wide, is an example of one of the simplest and most effective ways of rapid rendering. The buildings were first drawn-in with a delicate pen line; then the color washes were added. There was no attempt to imitate the true colors of the subject. The greens of the foliage are quite different from the summer colors of leafage, but by keeping the trees very high in key, interest is focused upon the darker hues of the old sheds which attracted me to the subject in the first place.

Country Farmhouse. This sketch is interesting in several ways. Note how the simple shadow pattern shown in the black-and-white analysis at the bottom of page 19 has been followed in the painting, although modified by considerable color variation. The rose tint that appears on the building at the left end of the clothesline is a pale orange wash which was first applied over all of the shadow mass; it was then over-painted with permanent blue and alizarin. I think the dark blue area at the right of the clothesline must be largely Prussian blue, a very dark hue that is useful where dark accents are wanted. Notice the free use of white paper on buildings and the ground areas between house and barn. Of course the ground could not have been so light, but how much less effective the sketch would have been had those ground areas been colored.

Bridge near Elkton, Maryland.

On the Jersey Turnpike.

Aldren's Farm, Putney, Vermont. This landscape focuses upon the great barn in Putney, Vermont, the home of my son Aldren, an artist. The hills in the background are in the adjoining state of New Hampshire which is separated from Vermont by the Connecticut River, hidden by the trees along the meadow's edge behind the barn. The sketch is actually half of a watercolor that straddles a double page of my sketchbook. The left side, not shown, is of the house, almost hidden by huge maples.

Greywold, 1951. The sketch at the top of page 39 is a view of Greywold, my summer home in the Berkshire Hills of Massachusetts from 1922 to 1951. The English half-timber style house was constructed of hewn timbers from an ancient barn. My studio occupied the smaller section in front, with a small bedroom on a balcony level above. The entrance gate was thatched with a local bush known as hardhack.

39B (bottom)
At Hooper's Cabins. This little trifle (opposite page) recalls "the end of a perfect day," the day having included a visit to the House of Seven Gables in Salem, Massachusetts. The view is a reminder of the hayfield adjacent to a cabin where my wife and I spent a night. What you see—what she and I see—is a glorious summer evening charged with the fragrance of new mown hay.

GREYWOLD 1951

at Hoopers Cabins   July 26 1952

Music Circus
Neptune N.J.

Sketched on a rainy day
Aug 14 1953

Music Circus, Neptune, New Jersey. This is a rainy day sketch made from my car, which was parked at the roadside. A brilliant star-filled sky had added to our enjoyment of a fine production of "Oklahoma" at the Music Circus the night before.

Farnham's Garage
Oct 2 1950

Farnham's Garage, Hampton, Connecticut. One's picture diary is likely to include some subjects that appear inconsequential but which nonetheless have much importance as reminders of pleasant days and rewarding associations. This old wagon-and-wood shed now serves chiefly as garage for Dr. and Mrs. Royal Bailey Farnham of Hampton, Connecticut, who live in the ancient farmhouse nearby. Dr. Farnham is President Emeritus of Rhode Island School of Design in Providence.

In painting this scene I first laid-in the dark areas of the shed interior with a grayed mixture of blue, red and orange, the blue predominating. The gray-blue sky was done with Payne's gray. Note how important are the white posts, wheelbarrow and other unidentified white shapes. The cadmium red boards at the right are a good foil for the green vine that drapes over the near corner of the shed.

House of Seven Gables
Salem Mass
July 26 1952

The House of Seven Gables, Salem, Massachusetts. This sketch recalls a day spent in Salem, the historic old city and port of entry on a peninsula in Massachusetts Bay. It was made from the garden where my wife Eve and I were served a good luncheon. The treatment of the tree mass on the right, where white paper plays such an important part in defining structure, may be of special interest to students. All colors are gray in hue except the yellow greens of the shrubbery in the foreground.

Boats at Tarpon Springs, Florida. Sponge fishing is the industry at Tarpon Springs, Florida, where these boats were moored, although the popularity of synthetic sponges has greatly reduced the importance of the industry. In a scene like this it is usually advisable to paint the sky first, superimposing the land areas upon it. The method of painting the sky can be clearly seen. When the lighter gray-blue color had dried, it was overpainted by a darker and brighter blue, probably a diluted permanent or ultramarine blue. The white masts of the boats were painted with opaque color after the sky was dry.

DEMETRA

Tarpon Springs
Florida
Jan 7 1954

FROM OUR HOTEL IN HARTFORD MAY 13 1951
HOTEL BOND

State Capitol at Night, Hartford, Connecticut. This sketch, made from a hotel window, is the result of my inability to get to sleep. Instead of tossing about on my bed, I decided upon this therapeutic measure. The sketch took about three-quarters of an hour, and as soon as I had finished, I quickly went to sleep. All is very gray of course, but the color at the time seemed quite faithful to the subject. The lighted tower supporting the dome is white paper. The park lights on the curving path to the structure were rendered with Chinese white.

June 12
1954

Elm

Campus of William and Mary College, Williamsburg, Virginia. This watercolor sketch was made in June 1954. The statue of "The Right Honorable Norborne Berkeley, Baron De Botetourt . . . Governor General of the Colony and Dominion of Virginia" stood at the main entrance of the fine Christopher Wren building. It is the focal point of my sketch. In June 1962, when I again visited Williamsburg, I was astonished to discover that the statue of the Baron no longer graced the entrance of the historic edifice. Entering through the central doorway, my wife and I noted a mimeographed release which explained that the statue had been removed to the basement because it had been seriously defaced by students.

Souvenir of Ocean Grove, New Jersey. My wife and I occasionally spend a few summer weeks in this "camp meeting ground" town on the Jersey shore. The architecture of the town includes many fantastic mementos of a bygone day. The curious peak-roofed structure which is the focal point of my sketch was originally the cupola of the house in which we were guests. (Now it serves as kitchen for the tiny cottage next door.) My watercolor was made from a private porch adjoining our room. The gray shadow tone which covers much of the sketch was first applied—permanent blue, alizarin, and a touch of yellow. The darkened windows were next, then the sienna roof, and finally the beach towel.

Church in Guilford, Vermont. Coming upon this church at
a turn of the road to Brattleboro, I was struck by the dramatic silhouette of the white-spired structure against the
darkening sunset and fall foliage. The gray-purple sky was
first painted, then the foliage was added. Although it appears
colorful, it is of course relatively low-keyed. Much of the
foliage was painted over the sky colors which in some places
at both sides were sponged out to favor the greens.

Manor Park, Larchmont, New York. This beautiful park on Long Island Sound is only three miles from our New Rochelle home and we visit it often. In summer months the harbor is the scene of great sailing activity. My sketch shows the harbor of the Larchmont Yacht Club. My intention was to focus upon the white sails by silhouetting them against the dark water and the hill behind. The sky of course is an important part of this picture. Warm gray cloud shadows contrast with the cool sky above. Although this seems to be a brightly colored sketch, actually all of the colors are quite muted.

Wagon Wheels, Banner Queen Ranch, near Julian, California. This ranch in the mountains northeast of San Diego is on the site of a gold mine owned many years ago by one of my wife's ancestors, who "mined it for ten years—until he went broke." Now it is a working ranch with accommodations for a few visitors. My wife and I spent several days there with artist Roy Mason and his wife Lena. The wheels stacked together were but a few of many which the rancher collected and sold to visitors. They made an amusing subject. This is only one of many sketches made during that outing. The dying live oak reproduced on page 56 is another.

on Banner Queen Ranch Jan 25 1961

Water

Water seems to present beginners with great difficulty when they are sketching in pencil, pen or other mediums that depend on line rather than mass. These mediums do not lend themselves to tonal rendering of large areas such as the waters of a harbor or a lake. The effort to simulate the value of a dark water mass with pencil tones results in rendering which looks and is labored. But in sketching we do not attempt photographic or literal representation, we resort to suggestion. Usually an expanse of water can be suggested largely by untouched white paper, provided there are shorelines, ships, boats or docks to turn white paper into water. This is demonstrated in the little sketch below. Note how effectively reflections serve to give reality to the impression of water. Turn now to the drawing of a canal in Venice on page 2 to see how simply the water is rendered by the dark reflections of the bridge and buildings. When dark reflections are broken up by horizontal or gently curving ripples, the technical effect is very telling, as you can see in the sketch of Gandria on page 51.

If your subject is a running or tumbling brook, the problem is different. That is one you just have to solve by experimentation. What you have to work with is the character of white foam shapes as water tumbles over a rocky bed. Always, when rendering with the pencil, the effort is to obtain the effect with as little massing of tone as possible.

Gandria on Lake Lugano, Italy. This old town, clinging to
the water's edge, forms a dark foil for the mountain that
looms up gray in the distance. The sketch was made from the
deck of a steamer that stood off the town for a few moments.
Representing large bodies of water is something of a problem. I've found that breaking-up dark masses with white ripples is effective.

Tumbling Brook. Except for a few tonal areas, mostly to indicate the direction of the flow, the water has been repre-
sented by white paper.

Trees

The drawing of trees is a subject extensive enough for an entire book. Indeed there are several such books that can be consulted by the ambitious student. Since there is room here to touch but briefly upon the subject, I shall point out what I believe to be the first and most important step in capturing the essential characteristic of a particular tree, which must surely be the intention of any artist who is inspired to draw one tree in preference to others.

In drawing any object whatsoever, the first creative act is analysis. The dominant structure and proportion must be analyzed before attention is given to detail. Otherwise we miss the mark entirely. However significant and interesting certain details may be, they will not portray individual character unless they *are* details of a prevailing structural pattern. So we have to develop the habit of searching for the basic framework upon which to hang details when we draw a tree.

A tree from its early life as a sapling is buffeted by winds which in time give it a certain "stance." Does it stand upright, or does it lean? Surrounded by protecting trees in the forest it may grow erect. If it has spent its life in the open, it answers the winds by yielding to their persistent pressures. In starting to draw the tree, therefore, one must establish its stance, and decide upon the degree of its deflection from the vertical.

Start by establishing the lean of the main trunk. In my analysis below of the tree on page 53, I have indicated this by a double line. Next, look for some geometric relationship of prominent branches. In my diagram these are indicated by A and B which form an angle that I have compared with a right angle (the dotted line). We now have two triangular shapes, C and D, with C the dominant area. The

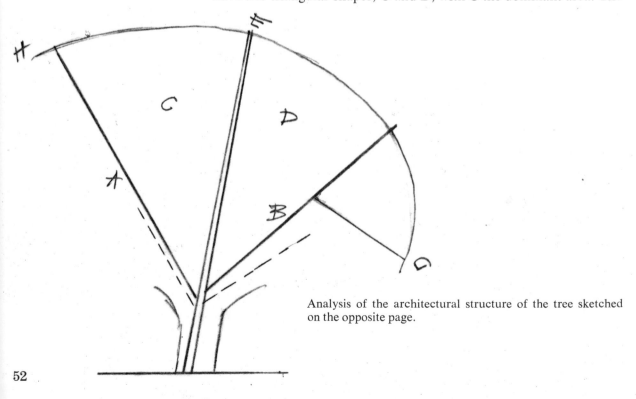

Analysis of the architectural structure of the tree sketched on the opposite page.

On the road to Sabina Canyon
Tucson Arizona
Feb 20 1959

A Great Tree in the Sonoran Desert, Arizona. No one was
able to positively identify this tree for me. Chances are it is
a mesquite. Anyhow the tree just made me do its portrait.
And a fairly big job it was—over two hours—since I was de-
termined to capture every fascinating structural detail. Actually there are two trees growing together. When this hap-
pens, trees have a gracious way of adjusting themselves in a
harmonious unit. Dark masses in the branches are mistletoe.

arc of foliage from E to G somewhat resembles a geometric arc. By letting the arc jump the foliage gap at the top of C—from E to H—we complete a contour that serves as a reliable guide to the tree's structural form. This very simple procedure can be applied to all trees, some of which may be more complex in structure. The inexperienced artist will do well to make a penciled diagram before beginning his drawing. It will take but a few moments and it pays off.

Having established the essentials of stance and the proportion of foliage pattern, decide about the treatment of leaf masses and make sure that there is suitable emphasis upon trunk and branches. These will appear light against the background of dark leafage in some places; in other places the branches will appear dark against the sky or against lighter foliage masses. Branches that are silhouetted against dark areas will suggest sunlight when shadows strike across them, as in my sketch.

The student of human anatomy spends time studying the skeleton, making many drawings of it in whole and in part. The skeletal structure of trees should likewise be studied. Make drawings of leafless trees and become familiar with the way in which branches grow from the trunk and from each other.

I have always loved to draw dead trees because they are so revealing of tree structure. And trees often die so beautifully. On page 56 there is a drawing of a dying live oak tree that I found on Banner Queen Ranch, near Julian, California. A variety of interesting techniques were used in that sketch. Note, for instance, how the pencil employs line along with mass in rendering the fascinating textural aspects of the decaying trunk and fallen branches. The drawing was made on a clay-coated paper which allowed me to scrape out light lines—with the corner of a razor blade—within the dark masses. Although this kind of paper is available in the larger art materials shops, it is not stocked by most smaller stores.

The drawing of palm trees on page 55 was also made on clay-coated paper with white lines again being scraped out of dark tones. I must warn you that palm trees are the most difficult of all trees to draw, at least I have found them so. Frankly, I had quite a struggle with them before I discovered how to isolate essential pattern structure in the constantly swaying branches.

The more one shares the life of trees by constantly drawing them, the keener the appreciation of Joyce Kilmer's rhapsodical tribute in his poem that begins, "I think that I shall never see a poem lovely as a tree."

Palm Trees, Delray, Florida. I drew this group of palm trees at the request of Eve who was especially charmed by their grace and luxuriant growth. The reproduction is considerably reduced from the original. The shorter trees are coconut palms which seem to be "sitting" on the ground. This sketch was made on clay-coated paper which makes it possible to scrape out white strokes from dark tones with the edge of a razor blade, as I have done in this drawing.

Palms
on Andrews Ave.
Delray Fla
By Eve's request   Ernest Watson
                          Feb 9 1963

Dying Live Oak Tree, Banner Queen Ranch, near Julian, California. While sketching trees in the canyon at this ranch northeast of San Diego, I was fascinated by the dramatic character of this dying veteran: the graceful, undulating sweep of the branch bowing down to meet an upturned fragment on the ground. I was also attracted by the great variety of detail: the contrast of the young growth in the crotch of the two huge branches, nourished by the soil of decay; the delicate intertwining of fine growth underneath on the ground; the rounded stones that point inward to the group. As with the drawing on page 55, this sketch was made on a clay-coated paper which allowed me to scrape out light lines from some of the darker masses.

Boat Basin, Rockland, Maine. I made many sketches in
Rockland. This one focuses upon an old barge moored at a
much littered dock. The foreground, which serves as threshold of the picture, comprises a jumble of logs, crates and oil
drums, all excellent grist for pencil or brush.

Ruins of
GLASTONBURY #1
ABBEY

Glastonbury Abbey, Glastonbury, England. Ruins, at least ruins of great buildings, have a sentimental appeal, and give the artist an opportunity to let himself go. Yet in such a ruin as this arched doorway one takes time, if he has it, to delineate with accuracy the architectural details that remain intact. One does so with reverence for the ideals that spared no expense or skills in creating glorious forms that carry their nobility to the grave of their decay. I made another drawing of the remains of the great nave, lifting high against the sky some of its graceful arches, while sheep grazed on the greensward beneath.

Street in Assisi

A Street in Assisi, Italy. This ancient hilltop city is one of the most sketchable that I found in Italy. At every turn in the streets one comes upon fascinating architectural surprises. Some I took time to draw with deliberate care, such as the one on page 33. Others, sketched in a half-hour, were rendered with bold pen line and wash (black warmed with a touch of sienna). Such rapid, "careless" impressions often have more spirit and a feeling of reality. The group of seated figures near the arch were women in the sun catching-up on their mending. They are placed at the drawing's focal point created by the converging lines of the street, the dark shadow of the arch and the concentration of light in that area.

Openings–Doors And Windows

In sketching buildings there is always the problem of rendering windows, doors and other openings that are very dark in value. If you fill an open doorway with an unbroken tone of black or gray, you will be representing a painted surface rather than dark space. Break up the dark areas with strokes of white or gray to produce a loose rendering that suggests atmospheric depth.

Windowpanes appear black or gray unless they reflect so much light from the sky that they appear very light or white. The mullions that divide the panes usually are very light and can be left white in the sketch. Avoid drawing windows mechanically as in an architectural rendering. Too much meticulous precision gives a mechanical aspect, while a loose, somewhat broken effect more realistically represents what the eye sees.

Memory Drawing

ʹMemory drawing is highly recommended as a drawing discipline because it sharpens the analytical faculty and teaches one to focus upon essentials. It contributes largely to the *seeing* process. In memory drawing we begin *seeing* by concentrating upon the subject's compositional impact—its over-all aspect rather than its details—as demonstrated by the following regimen that I have often given to my students.

When driving through the countryside you come upon a good subject, something you would love to draw or paint. Stop your car and just sit there trying to create a strong memory image that you can carry home with you without the help of a pencil notation. Don't draw, just look and try to determine what it is in the scene that attracts you. Don't attempt to memorize details; you cannot do it anyway. Ask yourself what it is that makes the scene dramatic. Fix the big elements in your mind, the dominant components, their shapes, their proportions, their relative importance. Plan your picture in simple masses. Don't try to remember what is within them: just the big things, the essentials, the over-all impact—no details.

Take plenty of time to form a definite mental picture. You will find when you get home that you remember the picture vividly. Draw or paint it from memory as soon as possible. The image may stay with you for several days but it will gradually fade away.

Having experimented with memory unassisted by pencil notations, at another time with a different subject try to supplement your memory with a quick pencil sketch. Study your subject as long as you wish, but allow only *five minutes* for your drawing. This will compel you to focus upon important compositional elements. You will have but a token picture, no details.

On your next trip allow perhaps ten minutes for drawing—no more—and then see how far you can develop the sketch when you get home. On succeeding trips take longer both for seeing and sketching, finally making a complete sketch on the spot.

This kind of memory study will train your skill in analysis. Its value will be appreciated later on during all of your sketching experiences. It is not remembering that really matters. The discipline is intended rather to sharpen your seeing faculty, a faculty which was so impressively implied by the late Maurice Sterne when he said to his students: "You mustn't draw what you see but what you have seen. One cannot make the best drawing when the vision is divided in seeing different parts at different times. Only when the vision is so coordinated that every part is seen in its true relationship to the rest does one have the right to indulge in drawing."

Degas, the great French master of drawing, said the same thing in different words: "After all, a painting is first a product of the artist's imagination, it ought never be a copy. If afterward two or three accents can be added, that doesn't do any harm. It is much better to draw what remains in the memory. It is a transformation during which with imagination in collaboration with memory you reproduce only what strikes your eye, that is to say the necessary, retaining forms and expressions. Never paint or draw immediately." This of course does not apply to sketching things you come upon and want to record in your pictorial diary, but the thought does point up a kind of skill that is useful, whatever you do.

Prickly Pear, Arizona.

Sabino Canyon, Tucson, Arizona. This sketch actually was
done in large part from memory. I started to draw the scene
from my car, which was parked at the side of the entrance
drive. I indicated the main contours and sketched-in the road
that crosses the viaduct and winds up the mountainside. Then
I began to render the detail, the giant saguaros and the rock
formation covering the slopes. But I didn't get far. The detail
was so confusing that I felt stymied! It seemed to be one of
those situations in which one cannot see the forest because
of the trees. Perhaps a subject of such vast dimensions was
just too much for the pencil. Back at my inn, however, I
looked at what I had done, and completed the sketch as seen
here. Evidently it needed what memory could allow, the
freedom from insistence upon exacting representation.

VIEW FROM SCENIC DRIVE LA JOLLA

ErnestWallWatson Fall 1961

64